hope
hunters

For more information, visit www.amy-lennox.com or email amybennett85@hotmail.co.uk.
Scripture quotations, unless otherwise stated, are from the ESV® Bible (The Holy Bible, English Standard Version®), Copyright © 2001 by Crossway, a publishing ministry of Good News Publishers.
Used by permission. All rights reserved.

Dedicated to my girls, Hannah and Emily.

"Train up a child in the way they should go,
And when they are old they will not depart
from it."

Proverbs 22:6

Enjoy reading this with your children.

Special thanks to my team who helped me get this book from an idea to your bookshelves.

Alison Kernohan who proof read and sought out all my mistakes. Gemma Montgomery who beautifully captured each idea I had. Jonny Lennox who formatted the two together so it became ready for you to enjoy.

Thank you so much for your help!

> **"I pray that God, the source of hope, will fill you completely with joy and peace because you trust in Him"** Romans 15:13

We are going on an adventure together.

We are going to read the Bible together and see if we can find reasons to hope. This world is hard sometimes, and it can be difficult in school, or at home, or if you feel sick, or if you are living between homes. It can be hard to find hope sometimes, even as a kid. So, I want to invite you to come on an adventure with me to discover hope in the BIble.

Hope is a word that we sometimes use to mean that we really want something to happen. Hope in the Bible actually means that no matter what happens in our life, we can be sure that God is in control. So, we can trust in God to help us through anything. Hope, real hope, comes from God as today's verse tells us.

Sometimes when we are going through something that is hard, or sad, or difficult, we don't always go to God for help. We try to do it all on our own. I encourage you to pray to God tonight and tell Him everything you are facing in your life, good and bad. He loves to hear from you! Ask Him to help you as you begin to search for hope in the Bible. Are you ready to begin our adventure together? Let's read this book for the next 30 days to find hope!

Let's become Hope Hunters.

DISCUSSION

What one part of your day can you thank God for? Did you struggle with anything? Did anything make you particularly happy? Tell God about it now.

CHALLENGE

Ask your parent or caregiver to help you read this every night for the next 30 days and see the difference you find in your life.

PRAYER

Thank you God for the hope that you offer to us. Help us as we search for hope over the next 30 days. In Jesus' name, Amen.

"We love because He (Jesus) first loved us." 1 John 4:19

Every night when I put my two daughters to bed, I tell them that I love them very much, because I do. I am their mummy and I will always

love them no matter what they do. Not everyone has someone who loves them like that in this life; however, did you know that Jesus loves everyone with a great deep love, including you!

The Bible says that Jesus loved us so much that He left Heaven, where He lived with His Father God, to come down and live on earth as a man. Not everyone liked Him, and when He became a man some people who hated Him ordered that He should be killed. So Jesus was hung on a cross and died.

People who were there that day thought He was killed because Pilate, who was in charge, told the soldiers to do it. But if you read the Bible, you will hunt out the truth. Jesus died because He loved us.

Jesus loves you hugely, massively, and forever, no matter what you look like, where you come from or what you have ever been told! Jesus loves you more than anyone else ever could. He will never stop loving you, no matter what you ever do. We can find hope in realising we are always loved by God.

Hope Hunters are loved.

DISCUSSION Does God love everybody? Even people who do bad things? Even if we do bad things? Yes, the Bible tells us so! Isn't it amazing!

CHALLENGE Tell yourself every day this week that you are loved by God, and believe it! Why not tell someone you know as well!

PRAYER

Thank you Jesus for loving me. Thank you that I am loved every day of my life no matter what I will ever do. In Jesus' name, Amen.

"I have called you by name, you are mine." Isaiah 43:1b

I remember the moment my oldest daughter Hannah was placed in my arms. When she was born the nurse handed her to me and I was so excited to finally meet her! She was so wanted and so loved already and I couldn't believe she was finally here. Emily is my second daughter, and I remember feeling just as excited when she was born because she was mine, and I already loved her so much. Both my girls were wanted very much.

Did you know that God wanted you here? I believe that God is filled with great excitement every time a baby is born here on earth, because He wants you to be here so much. He wants you to grow into a relationship with Him and He is excited for you to get to know Him.

You are wanted by God, very much. You were not a mistake, you were not an accident, and you weren't put here by chance. You were put on this earth by God, on purpose for a very special reason. He wants you. So, if ever you feel like no one wants you, or if you feel lonely, or sad, I want you to always remember that God wants you.

He has always wanted you and He especially wants you to be in a relationship with Him because He loves you very much! We can find hope in knowing we are wanted by God.

Hope Hunters are wanted.

DISCUSSION Have you ever thought that God wants you to be alive right now for a reason? Do you have any idea what God's plan for you might be?

CHALLENGE Tell yourself, and someone you know, that you are wanted and loved and valued by God!

PRAYER

Thank you that you love me, and that you value me. Thank you that you have a very special plan for me. In Jesus' name, Amen.

"For God so loved the world, that He gave His only Son, that whoever believes in Him should not perish but have eternal life." John 3:16

Do you like getting presents? A lot of us get presents for our birthday or for Christmas. Maybe you get a present on a day you have done something really brave or really special.

Did you know that God gave us a present a long time ago? There is a problem in this world called sin. Sin can be words, or thoughts, or things we do that go against what God tells us to do in the Bible. God knew that when sin came into the world, we were in trouble. Sin came into the world when Adam and Eve made the wrong choice in the

Garden of Eden by eating the fruit they were told not to. Because of sin we cannot be close to God or get into Heaven by ourselves.

So God gave us a present. He gave us Jesus into the world.

God knew that Jesus dying on the cross would give us the way to Heaven and allow us to be close to God again. What a present! But we have to come to Jesus, turn away from our sin and say we are going to follow Him with our whole lives to accept this gift God has for us.

When we follow Him with our whole lives, we get to be God's best friend. All our sin is forgiven and we get the gift of eternal life. That is the best present you could ever get. This is the biggest step in finding hope - accepting Jesus as your best friend and the gift of life He has for you.

Hope Hunters believe.

DISCUSSION

What do you have to do when someone gives you a present? What should you do with the present God is offering you?

CHALLENGE

If you already know God as your friend, why not tell someone you know about Him too.

PRAYER

Thank you God for the present of Jesus and for forgiving me if I believe in you, and follow you. In Jesus' name, Amen.

> **"Fear not, for I (God) am with you."**
> Isaiah 41:10

There are many things that can make us scared. Some people are scared of the dark, or a new school, or meeting new people. Maybe being away from your mummy or daddy can make you feel scared. Some children have a special item that helps them feel brave. Maybe you have a teddy or a blanket that you carry around with you. Did you know that Jesus does not want us to feel scared? The Bible has many verses that tell us why we do not have to feel afraid. Today's verse from the Bible is just one of them. It tells us that we do not have to be afraid because God is with us. God is always with us. We cannot see Him, but He is still with us. So when you go to school, or meet people, or are feeling afraid wherever you are, I want you to remember that God is always with you. In the dark, in the day, at school, at home, at the childminders, at church, at the shops - God is with you. So we can be strong and brave. We can find hope by realising that God is always by our side.

Hope Hunters aren't alone.

DISCUSSION When do you feel afraid? What have you heard today that could help you?

CHALLENGE Next time you feel afraid, alone, or scared pray to God and ask Him to help you.

PRAYER

Thank you God for always being beside me, day and night, so I never have to feel afraid. In Jesus' name, Amen.

"So God created man in His own image, in the image of God He created him; male and female He created them." Genesis 1:27

Do you like playing with playdough? My daughters love playing with playdough and clay. They love painting and drawing too. They love creating crafts and art projects.

Did you know that you were created? God created you! Imagine God spending time creating you. He made you with the correct eye colour, and hair colour, and shape, and height. He made you with the personality you have, whether you are funny, or clever, or energetic, or shy. God made you with the talents you have too. Maybe it is writing, or drawing, or music, or playing sports. God created you. God has looked at everything He has ever made and said it is all 'good,' but

He looked at people and said we were *'very good.'* God loves His creation, especially you. So never think that there is something wrong with you, or that you should be like someone else.

One day a young girl, called Amy Carmichael, had brown eyes, but she really wanted blue eyes. So she asked God for blue eyes, but He said 'no.' Years later she went to a far away country called India to tell people about God, and they listened to her because she had brown eyes. We can find hope in knowing God created us for a reason, with no mistakes.

Hope Hunters are created.

DISCUSSION Is there anything that you really like about yourself? Why not say thank you to God for making you that way.

CHALLENGE When you think of something that you don't like about yourself, try to remember that God made you that way, for a special reason.

PRAYER

Thank you God that you created me, with no mistakes, for a very special reason. In Jesus' name, Amen.

"A new commandment I give to you, that you love one another: just as I have loved you, you also are to love one another" John 13:34

Do you have a best friend? It is so good to have friends. Friends are easy to be with, easy to care about, and easy to play with. It is easy to love a friend because they are kind to us.

Did you know that Jesus gave us a very special command if we are His friends. If we have told God we will follow Him, that means we are called Christians and should obey what He commands us to do.

In this special command in today's verse, God tells us to love one another. God does not just say to love our friends, because that is easy to do. God tells us we are to love everyone, even if we do not really like them.

We are to love people even if they are mean to us, or do not share their toys with us, or push us in the playground. We are to still love them even when it is difficult.

We can show them love by still being kind to them, sharing with them, and being friendly to them even if they are not. Is there someone in your school you could show love to? We can find hope by loving other people so they can see that Jesus loves them too.

Hope Hunters love.

DISCUSSION Are people ever mean to you? How can you show love to those people especially the way God commanded?

CHALLENGE Decide one way you can show love to someone tomorrow.

PRAYER

God, help me to show love to others, even the people who are mean to me, so that they can see Jesus through me. In Jesus' name, Amen.

"God is our refuge and strength, a very present help in trouble." Psalm 46:1

Have you ever been in trouble? Have you ever felt all alone and scared? Maybe you have heard some bad news before that made you feel sad.

If we are God's friend, God is always watching over us and looking after us. If you have a bad dream and wake up alone in the middle of the night, feeling scared, God knows. If you have a fight with a friend and feel sad, God knows. If someone you love gets really sick or goes away and you miss them, God knows. God knows everything about us.

The Bible also says God is a safe person to go to and talk about your feelings with. God is a safe person for you to ask for help from because He is strong. He is a safe person to talk to because He always listens, and a safe person to cry to because He always cares. We can find hope in believing God cares for us.

Hope Hunters are cared for.

DISCUSSION What has made you sad or feel worried? Do you know how to talk to God about it?

CHALLENGE Ask someone who looks after you to help you talk to God about something that has made you sad or worried today.

PRAYER

God help me to talk to you because I know that you are a safe person. Help me know you are always with me. In Jesus' name, Amen.

"If you love Me, you will keep My commandments." John 14:15

Does your parents, or caregiver ever tell you to do something that you don't really want to do? Do they ever ask you to tidy your toys up or get dressed and you say 'No!'.

Just as your parents or caregiver ask you to do things, God has given us instructions to follow in the Bible. The Bible has everything we need to live a life that God will be pleased with, and that will allow us to have a life that is full of joy, peace and hope. It tells us how to love each other, how to follow God and how to hear God. Sometimes it can be hard to follow these commands but we can always ask God to help us.

We can choose to follow God's instructions for our lives, or go our own way. If we love God, we will want to keep His instructions because we want to make Him happy, and we believe He wants us to live the best life we can as well.

Sometimes our enemy, Satan, will try and tell us that God is keeping something fun from us. As a Hope Hunter, we know that Satan tells lies and so lets choose to believe God knows best.

You can find hope when you follow God and His instructions on how to live.

Hope Hunters follow.

DISCUSSION When can it be hard to follow what God wants us to do? What should we do when it is hard?

CHALLENGE Attempt to learn at least one instruction God has given us to follow and put it into practice. Ten of them are found in Exodus 20.

PRAYER

God help me to follow your instructions even when it is hard to do, because I know you want my life to be the best it can be. In Jesus' name, Amen.

"I will bless the Lord at all times. His praise shall continually be in my mouth." Psalm 34:1

Do you say 'thank you' when someone does something nice for you? It is so good to say 'thank you' because it shows we are glad for whatever it is they have given to us, or done for us. Saying 'thank you' helps people know that you are happy that they are in your life.

Praise means that we are saying 'thank you' to God. Do you know that

the Bible says God loves to hear us praise Him! He has forgiven the wrong things you have done, and He has looked after you. And so because He has done so much for us, it is great to say 'thank you' back to God.

We can't see God but we can be sure He will always hear us when we praise Him, any time of the day or night. Why not praise Him about something today? You can praise God in many different ways. You can draw a picture of something you are thankful for, write a letter of praise to God for all He has done for you or sing songs about how good God is. We can find hope by praising God.

Hope Hunters praise.

DISCUSSION What are you thankful for? Have a think with whoever is in your family about all the things you can be thankful to God for.

CHALLENGE Maybe you could draw a picture to show God what you are thankful for, or sing a song, or simply tell Him why you are thankful for Him.

PRAYER

Thank you God that I can praise you anytime and help me never to forget all the amazing things you have done for me. In Jesus' name, Amen.

"Don't worry about anything; instead, pray about everything. Tell God what you need, and thank Him for all he has done." Philippians 4:6 (NLT)

Both my daughters love to talk. They love to tell me stories about their day and I love to listen to them. Did you know that the Bible says God loves to hear your stories as well?

When we talk to God , it is called praying. It is a special time when we can tell God all about our day, about how we feel, and about what is making us worried or sad or happy.

Do you ever try talking to God?

It is so important, because even though we cannot see Him, He always hears us. Sometimes I am in the kitchen and Hannah is in the living room, but she still talks to me even if she can't see me because she knows I am still listening to her.

We can always talk to God about anything, and He will always listen to us because He loves us and wants to hear all about us. Why not try praying to God today? We can find hope by praying to God.

Hope Hunters pray.

DISCUSSION How and where can we pray to God? Maybe talk about different ways we can pray and listen to God in everyday life.

CHALLENGE Did you know you can make a prayer wall? Find a space and some sticky notes. Write prayers to God and take them down as He answers them.

PRAYER

Thank you God that I can always talk to you and you love to hear from me. Help me to talk to you everyday. In Jesus' name, Amen.

"The Lord God said to the serpent, "Because you have done this, cursed are you above all livestock."
Genesis 3:14

I have two little girls and sometimes they are the best of friends, but sometimes they end up fighting. It could be fighting over toys, or whose turn it is.

Did you know that there was once a fight in Heaven, where God lives. One day one of God's angels, who was called Lucifer, decided he wanted to be like God. So he tried to push God off His throne and take over Heaven. Now, God is stronger than any of His angels so Lucifer did not win. But God saw Lucifer's plan, so He could not let

Lucifer stay in Heaven. God told Lucifer he must leave. He will now live in a place called Hell instead of Heaven.

Ever since that fight, Lucifer is now called Satan, and has tried to get people on earth to follow him and end up where he lives, instead of where God is. So, God decided to send Jesus to rescue us and to make sure we could get into Heaven where we belong.

We must decide to follow Jesus. And when we do, we then need to stand strong and keep following, because Satan hates everyone who wants to follow God.

How do you stand strong? Read on tomorrow to find out! Hope Hunters know the truth.

DISCUSSION

Why does Satan not like us following God? Have ever you had Satan tempt you to do something you know is wrong?

CHALLENGE

Every time Satan tries to tempt you to do something you know you shouldn't do, pray quickly and ask God for help to stand up to him.

PRAYER

Thank you God that you are a strong God who loves us. Thank you that you have already won the fight against Satan. In Jesus' name, Amen.

"Put on the whole armour of God"
Ephesians 6:11a

Yesterday we were looking at how God has an enemy, and if you follow God you do as well. He is called Satan. The great news is there is no need to be scared of him, because God has told us what to do to protect ourselves from him.

In the old days, someone who was going to fight in a battle or a war put on a special suit to protect themselves called an armour. It was big, and heavy and strong so that anything that was thrown at them couldn't hurt them because it hit the armour and not the person.

God has told us in the Bible that if you are a Christian, we are to wear a special suit of armour from God to protect ourselves against Satan.

God says that there is a helmet of salvation which protects us against Satan sending us bad thoughts. A shield of faith which protects us against

Satan's nasty lies he can try and make us believe, and a sword which is your Bible that you can use to fight Satan with what God says instead. That is just a few pieces of the armour. Just as you can't see God but you know He is real, so we can't see the armour but we know it is real. It is full of ways to protect us.

Isn't God amazing, that He would tell us how to protect ourselves from Satan. So you don't have to be scared of Satan because God has your very special armour ready. You pray to God and ask Him to get you dressed in your protective suit everyday. We can find hope in having our full armour on.

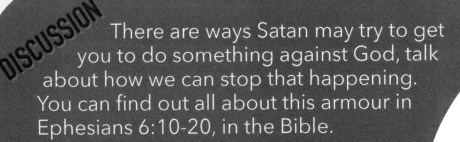

Hope Hunters dress right.

DISCUSSION There are ways Satan may try to get you to do something against God, talk about how we can stop that happening. You can find out all about this armour in Ephesians 6:10-20, in the Bible.

CHALLENGE Draw a soldier, look up in the Bible and label all the armour parts which God has given us to use.

PRAYER

Thank you God for giving us a special protection suit to wear. Help me to put it on everyday so Satan can not attack me. In Jesus' name, Amen.

" And Samuel said, "Speak, for your servant hears." 1 Samuel 3:10b

Do you ever feel like you are too little? It is hard when you feel too small to do something. Do you know that you are never too small, or too young for God? God doesn't have to wait until you are bigger or older to start speaking to you and showing you what His plan is for your life. If you have said sorry and are Jesus' friend, then God can start showing you what He wants you to do right now.

I know this because there was a little boy in the Bible who He once spoke to and told him what He wanted him to do when the boy was only about twelve years old. His name was Samuel. God called Samuel in the middle of the night by his name three times. Samuel thought it was Eli who he worked in the temple with, but Eli knew that it was God speaking. So Samuel said "speak

Lord for your servant hears."

And God spoke to him, and Samuel helped a whole lot of people hear God too.

Sometimes you can know what God's voice is saying deep within you so you just realise something is right or wrong, or you can know what He is saying through reading the Bible. So next time you feel too small to do something, remember you are never too small to hear from God or do things for God. God loves to use children in His special plan. We can find hope by listening to God.

Hope Hunters listen.

DISCUSSION

Why not ask your parents how they have heard from God before. You can discuss how God speaks and how we hear Him in different ways.

CHALLENGE

Take a few minutes each day to listen instead of having constant noise. Maybe go to your room for a few minutes and pray to God, and listen.

PRAYER

Thank you God that I am never too small or young to hear from you. Help me to listen to what you have to say to me. In Jesus' name, Amen.

"There is a boy here who has five barley loaves and two fish, but what are they for so many?" John 6:9

It can be really hard to share with other people, can't it? Did you know that God loves when we give to others, and especially when we give to God. There is a story in the Bible about a young boy who shared with Jesus.

There was a large crowd who followed Jesus for a whole day, and by the end of the day they had nothing to eat. One young boy had a lunch of five small rolls and two small fish. He could have kept them

all for himself, but instead he shared them with Jesus. And you know what Jesus did? He prayed to God and shared the lunch with everyone, in fact He shared it with five thousand men, and more women and children! One young boy giving his lunch to Jesus meant thousands of people got food, and saw Jesus do a miracle.

We all have something to share with Jesus. We can give Jesus our time and serve others, or we can give Him some of our pocket money to help others, or we can give him our talents of singing, drawing, or looking after people.

Whatever we give to Jesus, He can use it to help so many other people. Hunt for opportunities to give whatever you have to Jesus because you will always get more than what you give back again from Him!

We can find hope in giving to Jesus, and to others.

Hope Hunters give.

DISCUSSION
What do you have that you can share with other people? What talents has God given to you that you could use to help other people see Jesus?

CHALLENGE
Why not try and use your talents for God this week in church or at home.

PRAYER

God, I may sometimes feel like I don't have much, but help me to share what I do have with others, and especially with you! In Jesus' name, Amen.

"Gideon replied, "But how can I rescue Israel? My clan is the weakest one...and everyone else in my family is more important than I am."
Judges 6:15 (CEV)

Have you ever felt like you are too little to matter to anyone else, especially to God? Have you ever looked at people older than you and thought they are more important than you? Have you ever thought you need to wait until you're older to do something for God?

There was a young boy in the Bible who felt exactly like that. His name was Gideon. Today's verse tells us that he was from the weakest family in the whole kingdom, and he was the youngest and least important person in his family. So, he really felt like he didn't matter to anyone, especially to God. One day an angel appeared to him and called him a 'mighty man,' (Judges 6:12). God told Gideon that He had something very important for him to do, in fact he was going to defeat the enemy they were facing and rescue the whole nation. Imagine! Out of everyone that God could have picked in the whole nation, God picked Gideon to do the job.

little old me.

At first Gideon was really scared and didn't think he could do it, but with God's help he did exactly what God told him to and a nation was saved.

Never think you are too small to matter to God. You will always matter to God. He does not worry about your age, or size, or family.

So, if God tells you to do something, go for it. Because He knows you can do it! We can find hope by believing that God can use us.

Hope Hunters always matter.

DISCUSSION Talk about a time when you have felt too little to do something, and how you never have to feel that way with God.

CHALLENGE If you ever feel too small or like you don't matter, read this story again and remind yourself of how much God thinks of you!

PRAYER

God, thank you that you can choose anyone from any family to do your work. Help me to say 'yes' if you ever ask me. In Jesus' name, Amen.

"I can do all things through (Christ) who strengthens me." Philippians 4:13

When my little girl, called Hannah, started nursery school, there was one thing that she really struggled with. She really loved school, was good at making friends and enjoyed playing with the toys. But everyday when I went to collect her, the teachers told me that she was still struggling with this one thing. Sometimes she was sad about it, and sometimes she didn't worry, but everyday I encouraged her to keep trying. One day she did it! And we celebrated because she had managed to overcome her struggle!

Hope Hunters, keep trying with whatever you find difficult to

do that you know is good for you. God loves when we keep trying. The Bible verse today is a promise that says, we can do all things through God who gives us strength to keep going. So, if you are finding it hard to make friends, or to share, or to even cross that wobbly bridge at your play park, keep trying! God is watching you and He wants you to be able to do it.

You can ask God to help you, and He promises He will. And when you make it, you can have a celebration too!

Hope Hunters try.

What do you find hard to do at the moment? Tell your parents, or caregiver and see how you achieve whatever it is.

Keep trying this week at whatever you are finding hard! Ask God to help you every time you face it.

PRAYER

God, help me to keep trying things that I find hard because I know you love when I try and will always help me. In Jesus' name, Amen.

"I am the way, the truth and the life."
(Jesus) John 14:6

I went for a walk through the woods near our house today. It can be easy to get lost in the woods because it is full of trees and the path is very small and narrow. If I didn't stay on the path, I could end up far away from where I want to be, and it could take a long time to find my way home.

God tells us in the Bible that following Jesus is the right way to live our lives, He is the truth to listen to and He gives us life that lasts forever.

Sometimes Satan will want to stop you from following Jesus because he doesn't want you to go the right way, or know the truth, or have life that lasts forever. So it is really important to read our Bibles and pray every day. Jesus is the right person to follow through life and He will show you everything you need to know because He loves you very much! We can find hope in following Jesus.

Hope Hunters go the right way.

DISCUSSION

Ask your parents, or caregiver, if they have ever gone the wrong way in their life and how did they find Jesus again?

CHALLENGE

Start to read your Bible every day for yourself and draw or write verses that you really think would help you through life.

PRAYER

Thank you God that I can know the right path to take through life because Jesus leads me through. In Jesus' name, Amen.

> **"Noah did this, he did all that God commanded."** Genesis 6:22

I wonder if you ever wanted to do something that everyone else thought was a crazy idea! Did you ever want to jump super high on a trampoline, or fly in the sky? Sometimes we have crazy ideas that other people think would never work, and often they would never work.

There once lived a man named Noah. Noah was a good man, but he lived when there were many bad people. God wanted to clean the earth of all the bad people so He told Noah to build a big boat called an ark. Anyone who wanted to be rescued could come inside, with Noah's family and two of every animal. So Noah did what God asked. Everyone thought He was crazy, but Noah did not care. He kept building and did everything that God commanded. Noah obeyed God. Noah discovered God was the right person to listen to. After 120 years of Noah obeying God, the rain finally came and everyone was killed in the flood except Noah and his family because he obeyed God.

It is always the best idea to obey God, even if other people think what God is asking you to do doesn't make any sense. God's way is always right and good and will help you. If you read the Bible you will hear from God and it is your choice whether or not to obey.

Hope Hunters obey.

DISCUSSION

Has anyone in your family ever taken a risk obeying God when everyone else thought they were crazy? Talk about it together.

CHALLENGE

Have an idea book that you can draw or write down ideas. Let your parent or caregiver see them and pray about what God wants you to do.

PRAYER

God, help me to hear from you so I can obey what you want me to do. I believe that your way is always the best way for me to live. In Jesus' name, Amen.

> **"But Peter, standing with the eleven, lifted up his voice."** Acts 2:14

Do you ever feel shy and keep quiet, even if you have something you know you could say? It can sometimes be scary to speak up, especially when you are in a new environment or with new people. Even adults, can feel shy and keep quiet when they are somewhere new or meeting new people.

There was a man in the Bible called Peter. He was one of Jesus' friends but there was a time when he followed Jesus that he kept quiet about even knowing him. He was scared that other people would hurt him, and so he just kept as quiet as he could.

However, one day the Bible says that Peter was filled with

power from God. That day Peter spoke really loudly and clearly for everyone to hear about Jesus, and three thousand people became followers of Jesus because of what he said!

Sometimes we may feel shy or quiet, but you can pray and ask God to give you power to speak up for Him at home, or school, or to your family, just like He gave to Peter. He will help you, and you may just help other people become followers of Jesus too because of what you say! We find hope in telling others about Jesus.

Hope Hunters speak up.

DISCUSSION Was there a time you wanted to tell your friends about Jesus but didn't because you were scared? What could you do next time to help you speak up?

CHALLENGE If there is a friend you know who doesn't know Jesus, ask God to help you be brave and speak up next time you see them!

PRAYER

Thank you God that I don't need to speak up for you by myself, but you give me power to help me if I ask you for it! In Jesus' name, Amen.

"The Lord is my shepherd; I shall not want." Psalm 23:1

My daughters sometimes wake up in the middle of the night, sure that they have heard something moving in their bedroom, or someone is

under their bed. They don't feel safe and they call for 'mummy' to come in and protect them. I come in, we search round the room together and I make sure they know they are safe and there is no need to fear, because their mummy is here to protect them.

Sometimes in life we can feel afraid. We don't always feel safe. Sometimes our parents may move to different homes and we feel lonely and scared of the future, sometimes someone we love may get sick, or even starting a new school can make us feel afraid. It is important that we, as Hope Hunters, know who we can call if we need help or need someone to make us feel safe again.

David was a shepherd boy, someone who looked after sheep, who lived a long time before Jesus was born. He wrote songs which were called 'Psalms' in the Bible.

Psalm 23 tells us that the Lord is our shepherd. A shepherd protects sheep, looks after them, keeps them from trouble or danger and always makes sure they are kept safe and secure. The Bible tells us God does that for us. So, if you are feeling scared, or alone, or don't know who to turn to for help, you can always go to God. He is the best person to go to because He will help you find a way through and look after you as you face difficult things.

Hope Hunters are protected.

DISCUSSION What times have you felt lonely or scared? Have you asked God to help you? Will you in the future?

CHALLENGE Why not read the rest of Psalm 23 and see what else it tells us about God. Ask your parents to help you read it and explain it to you.

PRAYER

God, thank you for being my good shepherd who will always watch over me and look after me no matter what I face. In Jesus' name, Amen.

"**Then Abraham waited patiently, and he received what God had promised.**"
Hebrews 6:15 (NLT)

Have you ever wanted to do something right now, only to be told to wait? Have you ever really wanted to buy your favourite toy, only to be told you have to wait to save enough money up? Or, have you ever really wanted it to be the summer holidays, only to be told it is only a school day? Waiting is really hard to do, and waiting patiently is even harder! Patiently means that you wait without complaining or moving too fast. That sounds really hard to do, right?

There was a man in the Bible who didn't just have to wait a week, or a month, or a year for what he really wanted. He had to wait 100 years! His name was

Abraham. He really wanted a baby boy, and after 75 years of waiting God told Abraham that he would have a son. Even then he still had to wait another 25 years until his baby was finally born. Abraham wasn't very good at waiting patiently either, and so he made a different plan to have a baby boy. He found out the hard way that it was much better to wait for God's plan than to do things our own way, because God always knows best and wants the best for our lives.

So, as a Hope Hunter, I hope we will learn a lesson from Abraham to have patience and wait until God tells us the best way to do things. It might take a long time, but we can always trust that God knows what is the right plan for us!

Hope Hunters have patience.

DISCUSSION

Discuss what you are asking God for, and how hard it is to wait. Why not think of ways you can wait patiently until God answers you.

CHALLENGE

Practice being patient when your mum or dad tells you to wait, so that you can learn to be more patient with God when He says to wait.

PRAYER

God, help me to trust in you even if it seems like I am waiting a really long time, because I know you want what is best for me. In Jesus' name, Amen.

DAY 23

"Let us run...the race that is set before us." Hebrews 12:1

Have you ever had a sports day at school? What do you do when you have a race that you are meant to take part in? You run! I heard a story about a little boy who was taking part in his first sports day race. He was winning his first ever race, but halfway down the track he saw his best friend standing and stopped to tell him something. Everyone else ran past him. In a race you run, and you keep running until the end.

Did you know that the Bible says, if you are a Christian, you are in a big race. It isn't a race about winning, but the most important part of this race is finishing. Every day that you live as a Christian, that you tell other people about Jesus, or that you listen to what God wants you to do you are running the race. And Paul, who was someone who lived when Jesus lived, told us that we should never stop until we get to Heaven.

God has important work for us to do while we are here. If you are a Hope Hunter I want to encourage you to run this race and keep running until you finish it. Tell your friends about Jesus, read your Bible, listen to God and enjoy this life that God has given you the way God planned for you.

We can find hope when we run without giving up.

Hope Hunters run.

DISCUSSION How can you run this race the best way possible? Is there someone you can tell about Jesus, or give someone a Bible, or read your own?

CHALLENGE Why not pick up the challenge and tell someone who doesn't know about Jesus all about Him?

PRAYER

God, thank you for giving me a race to run and help me not to stop until I am finished with the course you set for me. In Jesus' name, Amen.

"The Lord replied (to Jeremiah), "Don't say, 'I'm too young,' for you must go wherever I send you and say whatever I tell you." Jeremiah 1:7 (NLT)

My girls will often ask me to help them with something because 'I'm just a kid'. Sometimes it can be easy to think of yourself as just a kid and so you're not able to do very much. Sometimes you're told that by grown ups, sometimes you just believe it because that is the way it seems. It can be difficult to be brave enough to tell your friends about God, or to do what you know is right when everyone else is doing wrong. When you're a kid it can seem very hard to be different, even when you know it is the right thing to do.

There was a young boy in the Bible called Jeremiah. One day God spoke to Jeremiah and told him to go and tell people what God said. But Jeremiah was still just a young boy, and as we read in today's verse, he was scared and told God he couldn't do it because he was just a kid. Did you notice God's response to him? God told him to go anyway because He had a special job for him to do. Jeremiah went and told the people about God and what He had to say to them, even though he was young, and God used him so much that two whole books of the Bible are all about what he did. Even though he was just a kid.

So, Hope Hunter, next time you feel too young to do something, be brave and remember what God did with Jeremiah even though he was young. God still says the same thing to you today, follow Him even though you are just a kid.

Hope Hunters are brave.

DISCUSSION When have you felt too young to do something? Does it make you feel brave to know that God doesn't think you are too young to do anything for Him?

CHALLENGE Do something that you have read about in the Bible, but have felt too scared to do because you felt too young. Tell your parents what it is before you do it.

PRAYER

God, thank you that you can use me even though I am still a kid. Please help me to be brave and do big things for you, because I know you will help me. In Jesus' name, Amen.

"But even the hairs of your head are all numbered." Matthew 10:30

I can tell you exactly where, when and the time that both of my girls were born. I am sure if you ask your parents, they would be able to tell you things like that about you as well. I know these things because my children matter a lot to me, and I love them a whole lot. So I know specific things about them. I know their favourite colour, favourite food, best friends and favourite places to go. Did you know this verse

in the BIble is talking about God knowing all about you! God knows all about you. He knows when you were born, what you enjoy, what you are struggling with and even what your future looks like. God knows all about you because He loves you! Maybe you don't have someone who knows all those things about you. Maybe you don't know who your parents are, or they are gone and you live with someone who doesn't know those facts about you. I want to tell you, God knows them all! If you have ever felt like you are not known by anyone, you are known by God. And He is the most important of anyone who could know you. He loves you more than anyone could love you. We can find hope by believing we are super precious to God.

Hope Hunters are known.

DISCUSSION Why does it matter that God knows all about you?

CHALLENGE Why not talk to God about things that matter to you as well. He knows but He loves to hear you tell Him.

PRAYER

Thank you God that you know me, inside and out and so I can always trust you no matter what happens. In Jesus' name, Amen.

"And He said to them, "Go into all the world and preach the Good News to everyone." Mark 16:15

I love talking to my friends. I love telling them what is going on at home, what I am doing, and I love telling my friends about Jesus. They often ask me why I believe in Jesus, who Jesus is and why I follow Him and I love to answer their questions. It is one of my favourite things to do.

In today's verse we read Jesus telling His friends to go into all the world and tell everyone about Him so they would know the Good

News that you believe in as well. If you are a Hope Hunter, Jesus tells us to do the same.

There are so many people who have never heard about Jesus

before, so Jesus left us here on earth to tell them all about Him. It is our most important job, other than loving our family and each other. Have you ever told your friends about Jesus? Maybe you could start.

You could invite them to your church, or a kids club that is happening near you. You could tell them about what you believe, or even give them this devotional book to read when you are finished reading it. Jesus wants everyone to know about Him, so everyone can have their sins forgiven and get into Heaven to be with Him. Will you start talking today?

Hope Hunters talk.

DISCUSSION Have a think about who you know, that doesn't know Jesus yet. What could you do so that they could hear about Him as well?

CHALLENGE Why not put what you have discussed in practice this week?

PRAYER

Thank you God that I know about you already. Please help me to start to talk and tell my friends about you as well, just as you told us to do. In Jesus' name, Amen.

"Like newborn babies, you must crave pure spiritual milk so that you will grow." 1 Peter 2:2 (NLT)

When you were little babies, you drank milk. That is all you could drink until you got older and could start eating proper solid food like your mummy and daddy. Milk was so important. It helped you grow up tall and be able to do more skills like walking and talking. It was important that people saw you were growing, because if you had stayed a baby all your life there would have been something wrong.

People who wrote the Bible knew how important milk was to help people grow. They also knew how important the Bible was to help people grow. That is why they encouraged people to read it, so that they would grow up in their relationship with God.

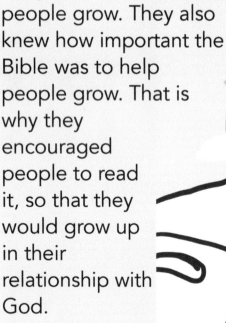

That is why I have written this devotional for you all to read; to help you grow in your relationship with God. When you read your Bible everyday and listen to what God wants you to know about Him, it helps you to be able to talk to Him better, tell your friends about Him and choose to do what is right because you are growing. So, I want to encourage you, after you have finished reading this devotional, keep going. Choose another one, there are many out there to help you keep growing. The more you grow in knowing about God, the stronger you will be when it comes to fighting our enemy, Satan and the more you will be able to do for God.

Hope Hunters grow.

DISCUSSION Why is the Bible important to us? How do your parents or caregiver read the Bible in their life?

CHALLENGE If you don't read the Bible everyday, why not sit and make a plan when it suits best in the day to read it and try and read it once a day, everyday this week.

PRAYER

God, thank you that I can grow and become more like you, because you have given us the Bible to read. Help me to read it everyday so I know what to do. In Jesus' name, Amen.

"One day the girl said to her mistress, "I wish my master would go to see the prophet in Samaria. He would heal him of his leprosy." 2 Kings 5:3 (NLT)

In Bible times, whoever was in charge at the time could take children to help them in their homes as servants. Today we are looking at a young girl who just happened to have been taken to be a servant for the man who was in charge of the king's army, called Naaman. Naaman was sick, and needed help or he could die. The young girl who was a servant in his house knew who could help him. Elisha, a man who knew and heard from God, who lived where she used to live could help him. And so, she told her mistress all about where he could go for help. They listened to her, and Naaman was healed by God! All because one young girl spoke up, and helped.

God wants us to help other people who don't know where to go to get the help that they need. Many people don't go to church or read their Bible, and some don't

even own a Bible. People who don't know God may go to your school, or your church even. They may even live in your own homes. It is our very special task, Jesus said, to tell other people how to find God and help them get into a relationship with Him. God wants us to help others so much that He has promised He will always be with us anytime we talk to people about Him, and give us special help as we do. So, I want to encourage you, Hope Hunters, wherever you are and whoever you know, help them! Help them find Jesus. Open your mouth and tell them, pray for them and encourage them to go places where they can find out all about Him.

Hope Hunters help.

DISCUSSION
Why is it important that we help other people find God? What can we do to help others find God for themselves?

CHALLENGE
Why not tell someone in your school who does not know Jesus, how they can get to know Him. Pray before you do, and God will give you special help!

PRAYER

Thank you God that I know you. Help me to have special power from you to help others find you for themselves too. In Jesus' name, Amen.

"My God sent his angel and shut the lions' mouths, and they have not harmed me, because I was found blameless before (God)." Daniel 6:22

Have you ever had to choose between doing what's right and what is wrong? I remember when I was a little girl in my last year of primary school, all of my friends were starting to say things that were bad, and I knew they were bad. I had to choose whether I was going to do what my friends were doing, or do the right thing and obey God. Satan would love us to choose to do what is wrong, because he loves it when we don't do what God has told us to. That is why it can be so hard to do what is right.

There is a story in the Bible about a boy named Daniel. Daniel now lived in a different land to where he was born. Daniel loved to pray to God and prayed three times every day! The king of the land had passed a law that everyone was only allowed to pray to him and not to anyone else. Daniel knew this was wrong and so he had to make a choice - would he pray to the king or would he pray to God? Daniel chose to pray to God and do what is right. You know what happened? The king threw him into a den full of hungry lions! Sometimes choosing to do what is right is hard, and can feel like God has forgotten us. However, God sent an angel into the den and closed the lion's mouths, so Daniel was saved. God never forgets about us if we choose to follow Him. God will always protect and help us if we choose to do what is right, just like Daniel. We find hope in doing what is right.

Hope Hunters choose well.

DISCUSSION Was there a situation you faced today where you had to make a choice? Was it a hard choice to make? Did God help you? Talk it over with a parent.

CHALLENGE If you have to make a decision, ask God to help you make the right choice.

PRAYER

Thank you God that you are with me always no matter what I face. Help me to choose right, even if it feels a hard choice to make. In Jesus name, Amen.

"There will be no more night. They will not need the light of a lamp or the light of the sun, for the Lord God will give them light. And they will reign for ever and ever." Revelation 22:5 (NIV)

Hope Hunters, we have come to our last day of our devotionals. I hope you have learnt so much about God and His special plan for you; how much He loves you and how much He wants you to follow Him in this life. But, did you know, this life is not the end for you if you are a Hope Hunter? God has promised that everyone who follows Him will live for ever in a special place He is making just for us, called Heaven.

The Bible tells us a lot about Heaven, especially in the last book of the Bible called Revelation. God allowed one of His disciples, called John, a glimpse of Heaven one day, and John wrote down what he saw for us to read. John said that the streets are paved with gold, and there are gemstones for gates in Heaven. He said that there is no night there because God gives us light for ever. He tells us that there is no more pain, no more times of being sick, no more sore tummies, no more times where you feel sad and no times when you are bored or frustrated. The best of all is that God will be with us there for ever and ever, and Satan will not be able to annoy or tempt us anymore! If you are following Jesus in this life, you can be sure that you will go to Heaven to be with Him someday. If you don't, why not decide today to follow Him so

you can be sure you will go there with us. You can look back at day four to see how to do that.

Hope Hunters have hope of Heaven.

DISCUSSION What are you looking forward to the most in Heaven?

CHALLENGE I have loved you joining me on our Hope Hunter journey. If you have any more questions, keep asking someone you trust. The answers are important.

PRAYER

Thank you God for Heaven and the promise that if we know you, we can be with you someday there for ever! In Jesus' name, Amen.

Keep hunting, kids!

BVPRI - #0006 - 221122 - C65 - 210/210/4 - PB - 9781399939324 - Matt Lamination